2003

Examining Issues Through POLITICAL CARTOONS

Abortion

Titles in the Examining Issues Through Political Cartoons series include:

Civil Rights
The Death Penalty
Euthanasia
The Nazis
Terrorism
Watergate

EXAMINING ISSUES THROUGH POLITICAL CARTOONS

Abortion

Edited by Mary E. Williams

Daniel Leone, *President*
Bonnie Szumski, *Publisher*
Scott Barbour, *Managing Editor*

GREENHAVEN
PRESS®

THOMSON
™
GALE

San Diego • Detroit • New York • San Francisco • Cleveland
New Haven, Conn. • Waterville, Maine • London • Munich

LIBRARY OF CONGRESS CATALOGING-IN-PUBLICATION DATA

Abortion / edited by Mary E. Williams.
    p. cm. — (Examining issues through political cartoons)
Includes bibliographical references and index.
ISBN 0-7377-1247-3 (pbk. : alk. paper) — ISBN 0-7377-1248-1 (lib. : alk. paper)
    1. Abortion—Caricatures and cartoons. 2. Abortion—Political aspects—
United States—Caricatures and cartoons. 3. Pro-life movement—United States—
Caricatures and cartoons. 4. American wit and humor, Pictorial. I. Williams, Mary E.,
1960–   . II. Series.

HQ767 .A153 2003
343.46'022'2—dc21

2002029936

Printed in the United States of America

Contents

Foreword

Political cartoons, also called editorial cartoons, are drawings that do what editorials do with words—express an opinion about a newsworthy event or person. They typically appear in the opinion pages of newspapers, sometimes in support of that day's written editorial, but more often making their own comment on the day's events. Political cartoons first gained widespread popularity in Great Britain and the United States in the 1800s when engravings and other drawings skewering political figures were fashionable in illustrated newspapers and comic magazines. By the beginning of the 1900s, editorial cartoons were an established feature of daily newspapers. Today, they can be found throughout the globe in newspapers, magazines, and online publications and the Internet.

Art Wood, both a cartoonist and a collector of cartoons, writes in his book *Great Cartoonists and Their Art*:

> Day in and day out the cartoonist mirrors history; he reduces complex facts into understandable and artistic terminology. He is a political commentator and at the same time an artist.

The distillation of ideas into images is what makes political cartoons a valuable resource for studying social and historical topics. Editorial cartoons have a point to express. Analyzing them involves determining both what the cartoon's point is and how it was made.

Sometimes, the point made by the cartoon may be one that the reader disagrees with, or considers offensive. Such cartoons expose readers to new ideas and thereby challenge them to analyze and question their own opinions and assumptions. In some extreme cases, cartoons provide vivid examples of the thoughts that lie behind heinous acts; for example, the cartoons created by the Nazis illustrate the anti-Semitism that led to the mass persecution of Jews.

Examining controversial ideas is but one way the study of political cartoons can enhance and develop critical thinking skills. Another aspect to cartoons is that they can use symbols to make their point quickly. For example, in a cartoon in *Euthanasia*, Chuck Asay depicts supporters of a legal "right to die" by assisted suicide as vultures. Vultures are birds that eat dead and dying animals and are often a symbol of repulsive and cowardly predators who take advantage of those who have met misfortune or are vulnerable. The reader can infer that Asay is expressing his opposition to physician-assisted suicide by suggesting that its supporters are just as loathsome as vultures. Asay thus makes his point through a quick symbolic association.

An important part of critical thinking is examining ideas and arguments in their historical context. Political cartoonists (reasonably) assume that the typical reader of a newspaper's editorial page already has a basic knowledge of current issues and newsworthy people. Understanding and appreciating political cartoons often requires such knowledge, as well as a familiarity with common icons and symbolic figures (such as Uncle Sam's representing the United States). The need for contextual information becomes especially apparent in historical cartoons. For example, although most people know who Adolf Hitler is, a lack of familiarity with other German political figures of the 1930s may create difficulty in fully understanding cartoons about Nazi Germany made in that era.

Providing such contextual information is one important way that Greenhaven's Examining Issues Through Political Cartoons series seeks to make this unique and revealing resource conveniently accessible to students. Each volume presents a representative and diverse collection of political cartoons focusing on a particular current or historical topic. An introductory essay provides a general overview of the subject matter. Each cartoon is then presented with accompanying information including facts about the cartoonist and information and commentary on the cartoon itself. Finally, each volume contains additional informational resources, including listings of books, articles, and websites; an index; and (for historical topics) a chronology of events. Taken together, the contents of each anthology constitute an amusing and informative resource for students of historical and social topics.

Introduction

F ew subjects continue to provoke as much controversy and disagreement as the topic of abortion. In the United States, much of the argument over abortion focuses on the question of individual rights—specifically, whether a woman's right to terminate a pregnancy supersedes an embryo's or a fetus's right to life. The debate is typically depicted as a battle between two camps: pro-life versus pro-choice. The pro-life movement asserts that human life begins with the union of sperm and egg and ends with natural death. From conception until death, pro-lifers contend, humans deserve to have their most basic right—the right to life—protected. The pro-choice movement argues that a woman's right to control her reproductive capacities should take precedence over a fetus's right to life. Although pro-choicers grant that an embryo or fetus is alive, they contend that it should not be considered a full person with rights until it is living outside of the womb.

A deeper look at the abortion debate reveals that the issue is more complex than the pro-life versus pro-choice split suggests. While the pro-life movement generally opposes abortion on the grounds that it kills human life, some pro-lifers grant that abortion should be allowed in cases of rape or incest, or when the pregnancy threatens the life or health of the mother. And while the pro-choice movement generally argues that a woman's decision to terminate her pregnancy is a private issue that should not concern the government, some pro-choicers believe that there should be certain restrictions on minors' access to abortions and on abortions occurring after the first trimester of pregnancy. Many Americans also "straddle the line" on the abortion question. Some, for example, may personally believe that abortion is wrong and should be discouraged but do not support legal bans on the procedure. Such a mixture of opinions is probably why Gallup polls consistently show that 50 to 60 percent of Americans favor abortion "only under certain circumstances."

Abortion in Ancient History

Because the abortion debate entails complex speculation on biology, ethics, rights, and the common good, it has never been a neatly two-sided issue. There have been women who sought to terminate their pregnancies since the beginning of recorded history, but the motivations to condemn or support abortion have varied widely with the cultural and political climate. For example, in the patriarchal cultures of ancient Assyria, a married woman who had an abortion was seen as violating her husband's line of descendants, and she was punished by being impaled on stakes without the dignity of burial. Conversely, in ancient Greece, abortion was often used to control family size, and the procedure was considered acceptable, as was the practice of allowing weak or deformed infants to die by exposure. Several Greek philosophers approved of abortion and passive infanticide as a means of population control and as a way of procuring physically strong descendants. Greek society's support of abortion was apparently motivated by the desire to protect the community by creating healthy offspring.

Religious Influences on the Abortion Debate

The focus on abortion as a rights issue—as opposed to a community-protection issue—has its earliest roots in religious traditions and theological debates. However, the various religions' views on abortion have never been consistent or sharply defined. While ancient Jewish laws forbade abortion as a means of avoiding childbirth, it was permitted if it was seen as necessary to save the mother's life. The Bible—including the Hebrew Scriptures and the New Testament—neither condemns nor supports abortion, but some early Christian writings define abortion as a sin. Church leaders during the first few centuries of Christianity, though, were more concerned about the possibility that women seeking abortions were attempting to hide the consequences of fornication and adultery. Many of them considered nonmarital intercourse to be a greater sin than abortion.

From the thirteenth century up to the present day, Christian leaders have held widely ranging opinions on the ethics of abortion. During the first millennium, some argued that male fetuses acquired a soul—and therefore became human—forty days after conception (eighty days after conception for females). Various popes believed that abortions occurring after such "ensoulment" were akin to murder and excommunicated church members who procured or assisted in such abortions. However, in the 1200s, the influential theologian Thomas Aquinas developed the concept of *hylomorphism*, which defined a human being as a union of a soul and a completely formed body. At the Council of Vienne in 1312, the church adopted Aquinas's theory of *hylomorphism*, which meant that (depending on what was defined as a completely formed body) the fetus was not necessarily considered human—and that abortion was not always a form of homicide. Yet another reversal occurred in 1854, when the Catholic Church formally accepted the principle of the Immaculate Conception. This doctrine held that Mary, the mother of Jesus, was without original sin at the moment that she was conceived. The theory's inference that human ensoulment occurred at conception rather than at birth provided the basis for later arguments about human life beginning at conception. In 1951, Pope Pius XII reiterated the Catholic Church's stance against abortion and explicitly connected this stance to a belief in a God-given "right to life":

> Every human being, even the child in the mother's womb, receives its right to life directly from God, not from its parents, nor from any human society or authority, no science, no "indication" whether medical, eugenic, social, economic, or moral that can show or give a valid juridical title for a deliberate and direct disposing of an innocent human life.

Although the Catholic Church later acknowledged that its theologians had never arrived at an agreement on when the fetus acquired a soul and became human, it advised its followers to "play it safe" by avoiding abortion altogether. From the mid-1800s to the late 1960s, most Protestant denominations also officially opposed abortion on the grounds that one should err on the side of caution in determining when human life begins. The Jewish tradition, however, has never recognized a fetus as having rights independent of its mother. While Judaism holds no one position on the ethics of abortion, most Jewish leaders have supported a woman's right to terminate a pregnancy. In addition, many mainstream Protestant denominations liberalized their stance on abortion in the late twentieth century. For example, in the summer of 1970, the Lutheran Church in America adopted the following statement:

> On the basis of the evangelical ethic, a woman or couple may decide responsibly to seek an abortion. Earnest consideration should be given to the life and total health of the mother, her responsibilities to others in her family, the stage of development of the fetus, the economic and psychological stability of her home, the laws of the land, and the consequences for society as a whole.

Abortion Laws in American History

Religious belief and the question of individual rights did not have a significant impact on American attitudes toward abortion until the latter half of the twentieth century. Early in American history, laws on abortion were derived from English Common Law, which prohibited abortions after "quickening." Quickening, the first sensation of fetal movement felt by the mother, usually occurs between four and five months of pregnancy. In an era before fetal development was fully understood, quickening marked the point at which the fetus was considered separate and fully alive. Moreover, quickening provided the only absolute assurance that a woman was pregnant. While a missed menstrual period was seen as possibly indicating pregnancy, it could also be a sign of disease or "unnatural blockage." A woman who missed a period could claim that it was the result of such a blockage and consult midwives or other healers to remove the alleged obstruction. In essence, then, pre-quickening abortions were allowable in most of post-Revolutionary America. Even when midwives suspected pregnancy rather than blockage, they felt no ethical or legal constraints in using techniques that could induce miscarriage as long as quickening had not yet occurred.

Although some locales attempted to ban pre-quickening abortions, the procedure became increasingly accepted as a means of birth control up through the middle of the nineteenth century. A growing number of middle- and upper-class Americans desired

11

smaller families, particularly as they moved into cities and as large families became more expensive to maintain. However, in the 1850s, the newly formed American Medical Association (AMA) initiated a vigorous campaign against abortion. This campaign was motivated in part by a desire to protect women from some life-threatening abortion-inducing drugs that were being sold through the mail and from "quack" doctors who performed botched abortions. But it was also inspired by a fear of business competition from reputable midwives and by aspirations to bolster the professional image of physicians. The AMA allied itself with the political opponents of women's rights and women's suffrage, arguing that readily available abortion threatened family life by encouraging "unhealthy desires" and by enabling women to evade their domestic and maternal duties.

Several developments in the latter half of the nineteenth century abetted the AMA's anti-abortion crusade. For example, after the Civil War, many Protestant churches allied themselves with abortion opponents, responding to fears that lowered birthrates among native-born whites coupled with an increase in immigration would lead to an Anglo-Saxon Protestant "race suicide." In 1873, Congress passed the Comstock Act, which banned the mailing of "indecent and lascivious" materials, including books and pamphlets containing information about contraception and abortion. By 1890, anti-abortion legislation had been enacted throughout the United States. Some states outlawed abortion entirely while others allowed therapeutic abortions—procedures done only to save the life of the mother.

Changing Attitudes

The anti-abortion policies established in the nineteenth century lasted until the late 1950s, when several states began changing their laws in the direction of greater tolerance for abortion. Throughout the early and mid-1900s, women had continued to seek abortions—either from illegal "back-alley" abortionists or from competent doctors who would find a pretext to perform "therapeutic" abortions. But by the middle of the twentieth century, when medical advances had made it possible for most women to carry their pregnancies to term, physicians found it more difficult to diagnose life-threatening complications that enabled them to prescribe legal abortions. Doctors could be second-guessed by medical review boards and face prosecution if they were found to be violating statutes. Consequently, in 1959, the American Law Institute proposed a new Model Penal Code that provided clearer guidelines for physicians and helped to counterbalance the restricting power of the review boards. The code permitted doctors to terminate a pregnancy if they believed it would critically impair a woman's physical or mental health, if the child would be born with serious physical or mental defects, or if the pregnancy resulted from rape or incest. In the 1960s, some states adopted all or part of the new Model Penal Code.

Other events occurring in the 1960s presented challenges to those who supported the most restrictive laws on abortion. For example, in 1962, Arizona resident Sherri Finkbine requested a legal abortion after she found out that the drug she had been taking for morning sickness, thalidomide, could cause severe birth defects. Her request, which was appealed to the Arizona State Supreme Court, was denied. She flew to Sweden to have the abortion performed, where a doctor confirmed that the embryo was deformed. Thousands of other pregnant American women faced situations similar to Finkbine's, particularly after an early 1960s' rubella epidemic swept the United States. Since children born to mothers who contract rubella early in pregnancy have a higher risk of birth defects, some women were able to obtain legal abortions. Others could not, either because of state restrictions or an inability to pay for the surgery. During this period, an estimated fifteen thousand children were born with disabilities. The AMA, which had lobbied so fervently for anti-abortion laws in the 1800s, now grew alarmed at what many perceived as a health crisis created by state restrictions on abortion. Moreover, a growing number of doctors recognized the unfairness inherent in the "therapeutic" abortions that were reserved for wealthy women and the back-alley abortions that were available to poor women. In the late 1960s, the AMA called for the liberalization of abortion laws, urging that access to abortion be restricted only by the "sound clinical judgment" of a doctor.

The problems with thalidomide and rubella created sympathy for the affected women who had been unable to procure legal abortions, and abortion became a subject of national interest. At the same time, several social trends were converging in a way that encouraged a significant segment of the population to challenge accepted beliefs and traditional values. The civil rights movement, a grassroots effort to garner social and political rights for African Americans, sparked debates about equity and individual freedom. A countercultural movement questioned the political complacency of mainstream society, initiating protests to demand free speech on college campuses and to oppose the war in Vietnam. Women joined the workforce in large numbers and became more politically active as they participated in civil rights and antiwar activism. Inspired by the civil rights efforts, a women's movement emerged in the late 1960s to protest the gender inequities that permeated daily life. Many in this movement saw abortion as one of the issues directly connected to their concerns about female autonomy and freedom. Arguing that access to abortion should be a woman's right, feminists sponsored teach-ins, petition drives, and acts of civil disobedience as they worked to reform state laws on abortion. By 1970, 60 percent of the American public believed that abortion should be a private choice, and Alaska, Hawaii, New York, and Washington had legalized all early term abortions performed by a physician.

Roe v. Wade

In the autumn of 1969, a twenty-one-year-old divorced woman named Norma McCorvey found herself with an unwanted pregnancy. McCorvey had recently lost her job as a ticket seller for a traveling carnival, and because of her lack of reliable income had granted custody of her five-year-old daughter to her mother and stepfather. McCorvey wanted to terminate her pregnancy, but abortion was illegal in her home state of Texas except when a woman's life was endangered by the pregnancy.

McCorvey's search for an illegal abortionist was unsuccessful, but it did lead her to two attorneys, Linda Coffee and Sarah Weddington, who were interested in challenging anti-abortion laws. Due to the length of most trials, McCorvey herself would not be able to benefit from any lawsuit filed by these attorneys, but she agreed to become Coffee and Weddington's plaintiff in a test case. As a representative for all women who had been denied legal abortions, McCorvey became "Jane Roe" in a class-action lawsuit filed against Texas district attorney Henry Wade.

Coffee and Weddington denounced the Texas abortion law on the grounds that it violated the Fourteenth and Ninth Amendments to the U.S. Constitution. The due process clause of the Fourteenth

Amendment guarantees equal protection under the law to all citizens and proclaims that states cannot infringe on an individual's right to life, liberty, and property. The crux of the *Roe* attorneys' argument, however, rested on the Ninth Amendment, which ensures that rights not specifically listed in the Constitution—including the right to privacy—are retained by the people. The individual's right to privacy should include a woman's right to decide whether or not to become a mother, Coffee and Weddington argued.

The lawyers representing the state (Wade) claimed that a fetus had legal rights that were safeguarded by the equal protection guarantee in the Fourteenth Amendment. As assistant district attorney John Tolles contended, "The state's position . . . is that the right of the child to life is superior to [the] woman's right to privacy." Roe's lawyers countered that "Life is an ongoing process. It is almost impossible to define a point at which life begins or perhaps even at which life ends." Since there was no consensus—scientific, legal, or theological—on when life began, the fetus could not be defined as a person that shared the same rights as the already born, Weddington argued. The judges of the Fifth Circuit Court in Dallas, Texas, agreed, concluding that the Texas abortion laws were unconstitutional because "they deprive single women and married couples of their right, secured by the Ninth Amendment, to choose whether to have children."

Although the Fifth Circuit Court had declared the Texas abortion law unconstitutional, that decision in itself did not have the power to end the enforcement of that law. Consequently, Weddington and Coffee appealed the case to the U.S. Supreme Court. Prior to the appeal, dozens of amici curiae, or "friend of the court" briefs, were filed in support of a woman's right to choose, including briefs endorsed by the American College of Gynecologists and Obstetricians, Planned Parenthood, and the New York Academy of Medicine. The "woman's brief," signed by anthropologist Margaret Mead, feminist theologian Mary Daly, and others, anticipated that the Court might focus on the legal status of the fetus, and stated that "even if a fetus were found to be a legal person, a woman still could not be compelled to nurture it in her body against her will." The signers hoped that the Court would decide that a woman's right to privacy and liberty always superseded the rights of the fetus, even if the fetus were granted personhood.

A Landmark Decision

In January 1973, the Supreme Court announced its seven-to-two decision in favor of Roe. During his reading of the majority opinion, Justice Harry Blackmun reviewed the history of abortion in the United States, pointing out that many of the nineteenth-century anti-abortion laws had been intended to protect women from a procedure that, at the time, endangered their health. That rationale no longer existed, Blackmun explained, since scientific advances had made abortion as safe or even safer than childbirth. Blackmun went on to discuss constitutional privacy rights, claiming that "this right of privacy, whether it be founded in the Fourteenth Amendment's concept of personal liberty and restrictions on state action . . . or . . . in the Ninth Amendment's reservation of rights to the people, is broad enough to encompass a woman's decision to terminate her pregnancy." The majority in *Roe v. Wade* also clarified the use of the word "person" in the Constitution, declaring that the word had no "possible prenatal application," and finding that the Fourteenth Amendment's use of the word "does not include the unborn."

In his dissenting brief, Justice Byron White expressed his aversion to the majority opinion, writing that the Court was upholding ill-advised "choice" over life:

> At the heart of this controversy . . . are those recurring pregnancies that pose no danger whatsoever to the life or health of the mother but are nevertheless unwanted for . . . a variety of reasons—inconvenience, family planning, economics, dislike of children, the embarrassment of illegitimacy, etc.
>
> The common claim before us is that for any one of such reasons, or for no reason at all . . . any woman is entitled to an abortion at her request. . . .
>
> The Court for the most part sustains this position: . . . the Constitution of the United States values the convenience, whim, or caprice of the putative mother more than the life or potential life of the fetus.

Despite *Roe's* guarantee of abortion rights, however, the Court also ruled that the state had legitimate interests in protecting the health of the pregnant woman as well as the potentiality of human life. Each of these interests was deemed to be more "compelling" as a woman's delivery date approached. So, while abortion decisions in the first three months (trimester) of pregnancy must be left up to the woman and her doctor, states are allowed to regulate the procedure in the second trimester in ways that protect the mother's health. In the third trimester, when most fetuses are viable (able to live outside of the womb), states may regulate and even ban abortion to protect the fetus, except when the pregnancy threatens the mother's life.

In essence, the *Roe* decision established a woman's constitutional right to choose abortion, but it also left open the possibility that state governments could regulate or restrict access to the procedure. The fact that the right to choose was not absolute—that it could be limited if the government found a compelling interest in doing so—set the stage for the legislative abortion battles of the 1980s and 1990s.

Post-*Roe* Debates on Rights

The national legalization of abortion in 1973 triggered debates on ethics and rights that have continued to the present day. In the spring of 1973, the Catholic Church–supported Committee of Ten Million began a petition drive demanding a "human rights amendment" that would ban abortion in the United States. Several similar amendments were introduced and discussed in Congress, including legislative proposals that would prohibit abortion even when necessary to save a mother's life. When these attempts failed, abortion opponents tried to organize thirty-four state legislatures to call for a constitutional convention on human life. Although this strategy was also unsuccessful, an energetic pro-life movement, composed largely (though not exclusively) of political and religious conservatives, gained strength during the 1980s and continued to seek out ways to turn the tide of American opinion against abortion.

Some in the pro-life movement express their opposition to abortion as an ethical stance that supports basic civil and human rights. Believing that human life begins with the union of sperm and egg, they argue that abortion denies a fetus its basic right to life, and hope to appeal to the conscience of a nation that prides itself on its protection of individual rights. In a 1997 speech, for example, pro-life Illinois representative Henry Hyde explained why he continues to oppose *Roe v. Wade:*

My feeling about abortion is based not on whether people should have the right to choose, but rather on when human life actually begins and the respect I have for the civil rights of all human beings. I feel that abortion is an act which violates the constitutional rights of an unborn child, who is helpless and unable to defend or speak for itself. I do not think that the murder of an unborn innocent is ever justified, and the instances in which abortion is considered absolutely necessary in order to save the life of the mother are very rare indeed.

Other pro-lifers waged legal battles in courtroom trials and state legislatures, seeking ways to limit the scope of *Roe* and help prevent the termination of unwanted pregnancies. Several cases that were appealed to the Supreme Court reveal this legislative strategy. For example, in the 1989 case of *Webster v. Reproductive Health Services*, the Court upheld the right of states to forbid the use of public employees and facilities to perform abortions not necessary to save the woman's life; it also allowed prohibitions on the use of public funds and facilities to counsel a woman to terminate her pregnancy. Moreover, the Court's 1992 decision in *Planned Parenthood v. Casey* allowed states to regulate access to surgical abortions—as long as no "undue burden" is placed on women seeking abortions. As a result, a majority of states currently enforces at least one of the following requirements: twenty-four- to forty-eight-hour waiting periods before women can undergo the procedure, counseling emphasizing the drawbacks of abortion, and obligations for minors to obtain parental consent before having an abortion.

Abortion rights supporters often contend that these state-level restrictions unfairly impinge upon the legal right to choose. For one thing, they argue, such regulations disproportionately affect young women and poor women, who are finding it more difficult to locate accessible and affordable abortion facilities. Furthermore, some pro-choicers see these restrictions—and the motives behind them—as condescending, insensitive, and unrealistic. As pro-choice physician Don Sloan maintains:

Suggesting that women need an additional waiting period flies in the face of common sense. It is as though this very heart-rending decision to abort were made on a whim by a woman on her way downtown to do a little shopping who just happened to pass by her local abortion emporium and decided to stop in and have one. . . . Does anyone really think women have abortions for the same reasons climbers scale mountains—because they are there? The decision to abort is always a true dilemma—one made between two unpleasant and unwanted alternatives.

No one is pro-abortion. No one is anti-life. No one. I don't think there is anyone doing abortions who hasn't wished at some point that the situations creating the demand for them would just go away. . . . But that would require a different world—one without poverty, rape, incest, contraceptive failure, genetic defects, maternal illnesses, unprotected moments of passion, or human fallibility.

Compromises Within the Controversy?

Although the pro-life and pro-choice movements continue to clash over the question of state-level limitations on abortion rights, some political analysts view the state requirements as providing a means of negotiation and compromise between pro-lifers and pro-choicers. The requirements are perhaps reflective of the fact that most Americans believe that abortion should be legally available during the early months of pregnancy, but remain ambivalent about later-term abortions, hastily made decisions on abortions, and abortions for minors. Law professor Michael W. McConnell maintains that a majority of Americans are pro-choice but favor government regulations because they "overwhelmingly reject the extremes." Furthermore, McConnell contends, "If the courts would get out of the business of regulating abortion, most [state] legislatures would pass laws reflecting the moderate views of the great majority. This would provide more protection than the unborn have under current law, though probably much less than pro-life advocates would wish."

Some segments of the pro-life and pro-choice movement have been willing to work together to reduce the often polarized nature of the abortion debate and to seek alternatives that each side sees as beneficial to women. For example, the Common Ground Network for Life and Choice brings activists together from both sides to find ways to reduce abortion rates without outlawing the abortion procedure. The Common Ground activists work to ensure better prenatal care, facilitate adoptions, improve access to contraception, and reduce teen pregnancy through programs that provide girls mentors and better educational opportunities. Feminist author Naomi Wolf argues that the Common Ground approach is the healthiest and most practical way to address the abortion issue: "It is time to abandon symbolic debates on Capitol Hill in favor of policies that can give women—who have been so ill-served by the rigid views on both sides—real help and real choice."

For the time being, however, the ethical and legal debate over abortion shows no sign of abating as activists, legislators, and judges continue to ponder if and when the procedure should be regulated. As the cartoons presented in this volume suggest, abortion continues to be one of the most persistently controversial issues in American culture and politics today.

Chapter 1

Is Abortion Ethical?

EXAMINING ISSUES THROUGH
POLITICAL CARTOONS

Preface

Central to the controversy over the ethics of abortion is the question of when human life begins. Many abortion opponents believe that life commences when a sperm fertilizes an egg cell—an event that creates a separate individual with its own unique genetic code. Terminating a pregnancy, in the anti-abortionist view, kills an innocent and defenseless human being—often for the sake of a woman's convenience or comfort. In a speech expressing his opposition to *Roe v. Wade*, the 1973 Supreme Court decision that legalized abortion nationwide, North Carolina senator Jesse Helms summarizes the pro-life argument: "There is no moment . . . when the fetus is not a human being. . . . It is now confirmed by biological science and by genetics that the fertilized ovum contains everything within it which will be developed in the individual human being. The genetic code has already established that individual's total physical makeup." For these reasons, Helms argues, the fetus is ethically and constitutionally entitled to the right to life and equal protection under the law: "An unborn baby is not a private affair between the mother and the abortionist. It is a three-way affair with the life of an individual person in the balance. The mother who seeks to kill her child for pleasure or convenience . . . and the doctor who is willing to perform the deed for a fee are not the most objective judges to protect the unborn child's interest."

Those who support abortion rights often question the contention that human life begins at conception. While most grant that the fertilized egg is alive, they maintain that it cannot be considered a person until it is able to live outside of the uterus. As geneticist Charles Gardner points out, "Fertilization, the injection of sperm DNA into the egg, is just one of the many small steps toward full human potential. It seems arbitrary to invest this biological event with any special moral significance. . . . The embryo is not a child. It is not a baby. It is not yet a human being." Others argue that even if a fetus were granted "personhood," its rights should not have "veto power" over those of an already born person. "You cannot have two entities with equal rights occupying one body," contends pro-choice commentator Brian McKinley. "In the case of a pregnant woman, giving a 'right to life' to the potential person in the womb automatically cancels out the mother's right to Life, Liberty, and the Pursuit of Happiness."

As the collection of cartoons in the following chapter shows, Americans hold a wide variety of opinions on the ethics of abortion. The question of whether a woman's right to control her reproductive capacities outweighs a fetus's right to life continues to provoke fervent debate.

Examining Cartoon 1:
"*Roe v. Wade*:
Landmark Decision"

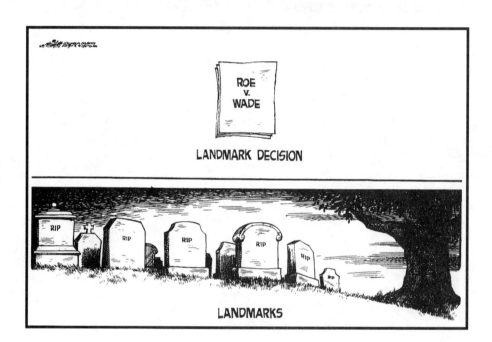

About the Cartoon

In 1973, the U.S. Supreme Court's *Roe v. Wade* decision held that a woman's right to privacy—including the right to end a pregnancy in the first two trimesters—was protected by the Constitution. Previously, abortion laws varied from state to state. Some states criminalized abortion except in cases where it was deemed to save a woman's life; others allowed abortion only if the fetus had severe defects or if the pregnancy resulted from rape. Women's rights advocates and liberal reformers see *Roe v. Wade* as a major legislative victory. Conservatives and religious traditionalists, however, often maintain that human life begins at conception and that abortion is therefore akin to killing or murder. In this cartoon, the artist expresses his disagreement with *Roe v. Wade* by focusing on a play on words involving the term "landmark." While *Roe v. Wade* is typically described by its defenders as a "landmark" court decision, the cartoonist suggests that the only real "landmarks" associated with the legalization of abortion are the countless unmarked graves of those who have been aborted.

About the Cartoonist

Dick Wright, a native of Los Angeles, California, has been an editorial cartoonist for several newspapers, including the *San Diego Union-Tribune*, the *Providence Journal*, and the *Nashville Banner*. He is now nationally distributed through the United Features Syndicate.

Examining Cartoon 2:

"*Roe v. Wade—* Back Alley"

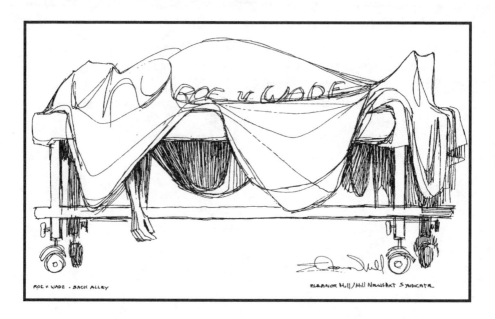

ROE V WADE - BACK ALLEY

ELEANOR MILL/MILL NEWSART SYNDICATE

About the Cartoon

One benefit of *Roe v. Wade*, pro-choicers often contend, is that it allows women access to licensed medical professionals who can perform the operation safely. Abortion rights advocates point out that before the 1973 national legalization of the procedure, many women who wanted abortions resorted to self-induced miscarriages or sought out illegal and unscrupulous "back alley" abortionists— dangerous practices that sometimes resulted in illness and death. In arguments about the morality of abortion, pro-choicers often maintain that it is unethical to outlaw medically safe abortion since women request the procedure whether or not it is legal.

This sketch appeared after the passage of laws that restricted abortion rights in ways that alarmed many pro-choice advocates.

In 1997, Congress banned access to privately funded abortions at overseas military hospitals for servicewomen, banned abortions for women in federal prison, prohibited insurance for federal employees from covering abortions, and denied abortions for Medicaid recipients except in cases of rape, incest, or life endangerment. Abortion rights proponents argued that these new laws effectively denied many women their constitutionally provided right to control their own bodies. Some pro-choice advocates also became concerned that the new laws were a harbinger of more severe restrictions on abortion rights—perhaps even an overturning of *Roe v. Wade*. In this cartoon, the artist expresses these pro-choice fears by depicting *Roe v. Wade* as a woman who has apparently died from complications of a back alley abortion.

About the Cartoonist

Born in Royal Oak, Michigan, Eleanor Mill studied art at the Corcoran School of Art in Washington, D.C. Mill illustrated children's books and textbooks for many years before she began drawing editorial sketches and cartoons in 1985. In 1998, Mill received the Global Award for Media Excellence from the United Nations–sponsored Population Institute.

Examining Cartoon 3:
"This Abortion Issue . . ."

About the Cartoon

One of the most contested issues in the abortion debate is the question of when human life begins. Abortion opponents often argue that abortion is immoral because life commences at the moment of conception, when a sperm fertilizes an egg cell. Conception, pro-lifers maintain, creates a unique individual with a full genetic code that is distinct from that of its mother. Many abortion rights supporters counter that the products of conception cannot be considered a living person until it is viable—able to live outside the womb—which usually does not occur until the beginning of the third trimester of pregnancy. Others maintain that since no one has been able to definitively prove when human life begins, the decision to terminate a pregnancy should remain the prerogative of the individual woman rather than the state.

In this cartoon, Chuck Asay mocks the pro-choice argument that "no one knows when life begins." He illustrates what he sees as hypocrisy among abortion rights supporters who would claim that a fertilized egg of an endangered species is a form of life while denying that a fertilized human egg, or embryo, is alive.

About the Cartoonist

Chuck Asay, a native of Alamosa, Colorado, decided he wanted to be a cartoonist when he was in the eighth grade. A two-time winner of the H.L. Mencken Award, Asay has worked as an editorial cartoonist for the *Colorado Springs Sun* and the *Colorado Springs Gazette Telegraph*. His work is nationally syndicated.

Examining Cartoon 4:
"Life Begins at Flirtation!"

About the Cartoon

The "morning-after pill" is a form of emergency contraception recommended for use for up to seventy-two hours after unprotected sexual intercourse has occurred. In 1997, the Food and Drug Administration (FDA) approved the morning-after pill for distribution in the United States, making it available with a doctor's prescription.

There is some controversy over how the morning-after pill works. The prescription is actually a series of high-dosage hormone pills containing estrogen and progesterone, given in two doses twelve hours apart. While its supporters maintain that the hormones inhibit ovulation, critics argue that the pills can also prevent fertilized eggs from implanting into the uterus. Consequently, some pro-life advocates maintain that emergency contraception sometimes induces chemical abortion. They define the morning-after pill as an "abortifacient," or potentially abortion causing, prescription.

This cartoon parodies the stance of abortion opponents who condemn emergency contraception. Ann Telnaes depicts a pro-life advocate as not only strident and obnoxious, but also irrational enough to argue that human life begins even *before* conception. By using exaggeration, the cartoonist suggests that the pro-life opposition to the morning-after pill is illogical and absurd.

About the Cartoonist

A native of Sweden, Ann Telnaes studied character animation at the California Institute of the Arts. Before beginning her career as an editorial cartoonist, she worked for several years as a designer for Walt Disney Imagineering. Her political cartoons have appeared in the *Chicago Tribune*, the *Washington Post*, the *Los Angeles Times*, the *Baltimore Sun*, the *New York Times*, and *USA Today*. In 2001, Telnaes won the Pulitzer Prize for editorial cartooning.

Examining Cartoon 5:
"Terrible! Imagine the U.S. Government . . ."

About the Cartoon

Pro-life advocates often maintain that pro-choice arguments for abortion rights echo historical justifications for slavery. Some abortion opponents contend, for example, that the assertion that an embryo or fetus does not have a right to life because it is not yet a person is comparable to a slaveholder's claim that blacks do not have rights because they are not fully human.

This cartoon portrays the liberal pro-choice opinion as fickle and inconsistent. The artist argues that pro-choice advocates can be outraged that the U.S. government previously allowed blacks to be treated inhumanely—yet fail to see that their own beliefs about the fetus being "not human" and "the property of its owner" are just as merciless.

About the Cartoonist

Jim Ridings is the author of several comic book series, including *Cheese Weasel, Catnip*, and *The Fatt Family.* He has also published two books of satirical political cartoons: *The Politically Incorrect Cheese Weasel* and *Ashpile.*

Examining Cartoon 6:

"*No* Abortions Under *Any* Circumstances"

"Your life is in danger? So what?!
We're only concerned with the sanctity of life!"

About the Cartoon

Religious conservatives and others who champion traditional moral values generally maintain that deliberate abortion is always wrong because it violates the sanctity of life. The official opinion of the Catholic Church, for example, holds that human life is "sacred and inviolable" from conception until natural death and that Christians must never "intentionally kill, or collude in the killing of, any innocent human life, no matter how broken, unformed, disabled or desperate that life may seem." The Catholic Church does permit a procedure referred to as "indirect abortion"—which occurs when the primary intention is to save the mother's life and involves no purposeful killing of the embryo or fetus. Such a situation might arise when a pregnant woman has malignant uterine cancer and must have her uterus removed, resulting in the unintentional death of the fetus.

Pro-choice advocates, however, view the "sanctity of life" argument as unconvincing because they feel it does not take the pregnant woman's life and health into full consideration. A woman could have a chronic illness, such as diabetes, epilepsy, or heart disease, that might jeopardize her life if she continued a pregnancy to term. In such situations, abortion rights supporters contend, it would probably be better for the woman to have a direct abortion early in her pregnancy rather than wait until life-threatening complications arise. Pro-choicers maintain that such difficult decisions can only be made by a woman and her doctor.

This cartoon paints the sanctity-of-life argument as self-contradictory. The cartoonist uses irony by depicting those who claim to support life as indifferent to the life of the woman. He suggests that the pro-life opposition to abortion is harsh and narrow-minded because it fails to acknowledge the sanctity of a woman's life or the complexities that are often involved in the choice to end a pregnancy.

About the Cartoonist

Bruce Beattie studied at the Art Center College of Design in Los Angeles before working as an editorial cartoonist—first for the *Honolulu Advertiser* and then for the *Daytona Beach News-Journal*. Beattie has served as president of the National Cartoonists Society and as a board member of the Association of American Editorial Cartoonists. His awards include the Florida Society of Professional Journalists' Sunshine State Award for Excellence in Editorial Cartooning and the Florida Press Club's Award for Excellence in Journalism.

Chapter 2

Should Abortion Rights Be Restricted or Protected?

Preface

E ileen Roberts was at a loss when her fourteen-year-old daughter sunk into a deep depression. Searching for answers, Roberts was shocked to discover an abortion clinic questionnaire underneath her daughter's pillow. The girl had recently terminated her pregnancy in a neighboring state that did not require parental consent for minors' abortions. As a result of the ensuing depression, Roberts's daughter had to be hospitalized, at which time doctors discovered that the abortion was incomplete and would require surgery to repair the damage done by the abortionist. Ironically, Roberts recalls, her daughter could not have had this reparative surgery without a signed parental consent form.

Roberts's experience reveals why many people support laws that require teens to notify their parents or obtain their parents' consent before having an abortion. In the 1992 case of *Planned Parenthood v. Casey*, the Supreme Court upheld the right of states to pass laws restricting access to abortions—as long as no "undue burden" was placed on women seeking the procedure. As a result of *Casey*, most states currently have parental consent laws—although some states allow a minor to get an abortion without parental notification if a judge or specified health professional waives the requirement. Florida representative Charles T. Canady maintains that parental consent laws are necessary because without them, "the risks to the child's health significantly increases. Only parents have knowledge of their daughter's prior medical and psychological history, and would, for instance, be able to alert the abortionist of allergies to anesthesia and medication and provide authorization for the release of pertinent data from family physicians."

Many pro-choicers, however, are opposed to parental consent laws. Pediatrician Jonathan Klein, for example, argues that such laws severely limit teen access to safe and confidential abortions. While he grants that teens should be encouraged to discuss an abortion decision with their parents, he recognizes that some girls face rejection or abuse if their parents learn about their pregnancies. "All too often, . . . young women know that their parents would be overwhelmed, angry, distraught, or disappointed if they knew about the crisis pregnancy. Fear of emotional or physical abuse, including being thrown out of the house, are among the major reasons teenagers say they are afraid to tell their parents about a pregnancy." The possibility of parental disapproval also increases the risk that teens will choose desperate measures to maintain the confidentiality of their pregnancies, Klein maintains: "They may run away from home, obtain a 'back alley' abortion, or resort to a self-induced abortion." Faced with these scenarios, Klein and many other medical professionals do not support strict enforcement of parental notification laws.

Parental consent requirements and other state laws that regulate access to abortions have been the source of most of the recent legislative battles concerning abortion rights. The cartoonists in the following chapter offer further commentary on the question of whether abortion rights should be restricted or protected.

Examining Cartoon 1:
"Legal but Impossible"

About the Cartoon

The U.S. Supreme Court's 1992 decision in *Planned Parenthood v. Casey* allowed states to regulate access to abortions as long as no "undue burden" is placed on women who wish to have an abortion. As a result, many state legislatures passed laws during the 1990s that required women to fulfill certain requirements before obtaining an abortion. Currently, a majority of states enforces at least one of the following regulations: twenty-four- to forty-eight-hour waiting periods before women can undergo the operation, counseling focusing on the drawbacks of abortion, obligations for minors to notify their parents or obtain their parents' consent before having an abortion, and bans on the surgery at government-funded facilities.

Many pro-choice advocates see these regulations as unfairly restricting a woman's legal right to have an abortion. This cartoonist argues that while abortion remains legal, state regulations can make the procedure so difficult to obtain that it is almost as if abortion were illegal. The term "Shrub" is an intentionally disparaging reference to abortion opponent George W. Bush, who had been president for a little over a year when this cartoon was first published. The "rules" that the two characters discuss are of course nonexistent—but offer sarcastic commentary on the potential future of abortion rights under an anti-abortion president.

About the Cartoonist

Stephanie McMillan graduated from New York University in 1987 with a degree in film animation. McMillan is the creator of the comic strip series *Minimum Security*, which appears in several journals, including *Redzine, Against the Current, Humanist, off our backs*, the *San Francisco Bay-Guardian*, and Z magazine. In 1994 and 1997, she received first place awards from the Florida Press Club for excellence in editorial cartooning.

Examining Cartoon 2:
"Partial-Birth Abortion Remains Legal . . ."

PARTIAL-BIRTH ABORTION REMAINS LEGAL...

Mike Shelton ©1996
THE ORANGE COUNTY REGISTER

About the Cartoon

This cartoon comments on a controversial form of second-trimester abortion known as intact dilation and extraction, or "D&X." Referred to as "partial-birth abortion" by its opponents, D&X is performed on women who are between twenty and twenty-four weeks pregnant, ostensibly when the fetus has severe defects or when the pregnancy endangers the mother's health. During the procedure, the physician delivers all but the head of the fetus from the uterus, then uses scissors to cut a hole in the base of the fetus's skull so that its brain can be removed. This allows the fetus's head to collapse so that it can more easily pass through the cervical opening.

The public is divided over the issue of late-term abortions. Critics contend that at twenty-four weeks, more than 50 percent of fetuses are able to live outside of the womb—and many people, including some who generally identify themselves as pro-choice, see D&X as an immoral procedure akin to infanticide. Between 1995 and 2000, Congress passed several bills attempting to impose a nationwide ban on D&X abortions, but each of these bills was vetoed by pro-choice president Bill Clinton.

In this cartoon, the image of a guillotine on one end of an operating table, with a trash can below it to catch soon-to-be-discarded body parts, suggests that the D&X procedure is crude and gruesome—more comparable to a primitive form of execution than surgery.

About the Cartoonist

Mike Shelton is the editorial cartoonist for the *Orange County (California) Register.*

Shelton. © 1996 by the *Orange County Register.* Reprinted by permission of King Features Syndicate.

Examining Cartoon 3:

"RU-486: FDA Approved"

About the Cartoon

In the year 2000, the Food and Drug Administration (FDA) approved the sale of RU-486, a pill that induces nonsurgical abortion during the first seven weeks of pregnancy. RU-486 is actually a two-drug combination: mifepristone causes the uterus to shed its lining and dislodge the embryo; then misoprostol, taken two days later, causes contractions that help to expel the remaining tissue.

This cartoon makes its point by highlighting what some see as contradictions in the FDA's labeling system. While alcohol and tobacco products are required to have warning labels stating that such products may harm unborn children, RU-486, which actually kills embryos, is depicted with an "FDA Approved" label. The cartoonist employs irony by placing a bottle of wine and a pack of cigarettes right next to a bottle of RU-486. The implication is that governmental policies are badly skewed if they allow a product such as RU-486 on the market.

About the Cartoonist

Nationally syndicated cartoonist Chip Bok is the editorial cartoonist for the *Akron (Ohio) Beacon Journal* and a regular contributing cartoonist for *Reason* magazine. His awards include the 1993 H.L. Mencken Award for editorial cartooning and the 1995 National Cartoonist Society award.

Examining Cartoon 4:
"RU-486"

About the Cartoon

Abortion rights supporters welcomed the Food and Drug Administration approval of RU-486, the "abortion pill," in September 2000. According to the National Abortion and Reproductive Rights Action League (NARAL), 95 percent of women who have used RU-486 would recommend the method to others, while 91 percent would choose it again if necessary. NARAL maintains that many women prefer an RU-486 abortion over traditional abortion because the pill's two-drug combination, which induces miscarriage during the first seven weeks of pregnancy, is a private and noninvasive medical procedure.

This pro-choice cartoon illustrates what many see as another significant benefit of the abortion pill: Women seeking the prescription for RU-486 are less likely to encounter harassment from anti-abortion activists who target clinics where surgical abortions are performed. In addition, by drawing the three abortion protesters with anxious facial expressions, the cartoonist suggests that RU-486 poses a threat to the anti-abortion movement.

About the Cartoonist

Steve Greenberg received an art degree from California State University in Long Beach before working as an editorial cartoonist for the Los Angeles *Daily News* from 1978 to 1984. Between 1985 and 2000 he worked as an artist and cartoonist for the *Seattle Post-Intelligencer*. Greenberg's honors include the 1994 Global Media Award for cartoons about overpopulation and the 1991 Cartoonists Northwest Cartoonist of the Year "Toonie" Award. He now works as an editorial cartoonist and graphic artist in San Francisco, drawing for the *San Francisco Examiner, Mad Magazine*, and other publications.

Examining Cartoon 5:
"Women's Clinic"

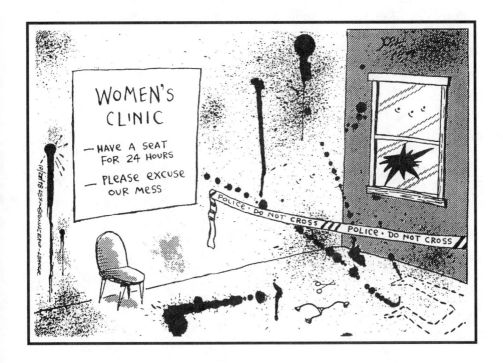

About the Cartoon

This darkly satirical sketch of a blood-spattered and bullet-pocked women's clinic captures some of the frustration expressed by pro-choice advocates who confront anti-abortion violence and legislation that restricts abortion rights. The stethoscope, scissors, and body outline imply that a physician has been killed. The empty chair underneath a sign that states "Have a seat for 24 hours" represents pro-choice indignation with state laws that regulate access to abortion—made to seem all the more outrageous with this cartoon's contention that a woman who wishes to obtain an abortion at a clinic will face threats to her life.

About the Cartoonist

Joel Pett has been the editorial cartoonist at the *Lexington (Kentucky) Herald-Leader* since 1984. His cartoons have appeared in hundreds of periodicals nationwide, including the *New York Times*, *Los Angeles Times*, the *Boston Globe*, *USA Today*, *Ms.*, and *Discover*. His honors include the 2000 Pulitzer Prize for editorial cartoons and the 1995 Global Media Award for cartoons on population issues.

Examining Cartoon 6:
"Ethics Debate of the Future"

About the Cartoon

In June 2000, the U.S. Supreme Court struck down a Nebraska ban on late-term dilation and extraction (D&X) abortions, referred to as "partial-birth" abortions by its critics because the fetus is partially delivered before its brain is removed to complete the operation.

Abortion opponents saw this court ruling as a gross infringement on the right to life, especially in light of a survey that revealed that the majority of late-term abortions are not done in response to extreme medical conditions, but on healthy mothers and on potentially viable fetuses with only minor birth defects.

Through exaggeration, this cartoon dramatizes what many pro-life advocates see as the "slippery slope" of abortion rights. With partial-birth abortion remaining legal, this cartoonist envisions a future in which the right to life has been so undermined that ethicists can conceivably argue about "post-birth" abortions.

About the Cartoonist

Joel Kauffman is the creator of *Pontius' Puddle*, a comic strip series that editorializes on issues from a traditional Christian point of view.

Chapter 3

Should Protesters Target Abortion Providers?

EXAMINING ISSUES THROUGH
POLITICAL CARTOONS

Preface

Throughout the 1980s and 1990s, abortion opponents have adopted several kinds of protest tactics in an attempt to dissuade women from having abortions. The mainstream pro-life movement endorses the practice of demonstrating, leafleting, and holding prayer vigils outside of abortion clinics, believing that such strategies might encourage women to change their minds about terminating their pregnancies. Radical anti-abortion groups, however, have implicitly or explicitly sanctioned the use of more extreme protest tactics, such as blockades, vandalism, bombings and arsons of abortion clinics, threats and acts of violence against abortion providers (including the murder of abortionists), and the publicizing of names and addresses of abortion providers and abortion seekers. The year 1993 was an exceptionally active year for radical abortion opponents, with 452 acts of violence against abortion providers and 66 clinic blockades. In 2001, only 2 clinic blockades occurred, but there were 379 acts of violence against abortion providers—including 283 anthrax threats.

In 1994, largely in response to the number of violent incidents against abortion providers, the Freedom of Access to Clinic Entrances Act (FACE) was signed into law. FACE prohibits the actions of anyone who "by force or threat of force or by physical obstruction, intentionally injures, intimidates or interferes with or attempts to injure, intimidate or interfere with any person . . . obtaining or providing reproductive health services." The legislation received support from both abortion rights proponents and opponents. Pro-life Nevada senator Harry Reid stated that although he opposed abortion, he supported FACE because its intent was "not to restrict the rights of people to demonstrate but to protect the rights of people to be free from the fear of violence against them." Others, however, contend that FACE violates constitutional rights to freedom of speech and freedom of religion. They see the outlawing of clinic blockades, for example, as similar to the sanctions taken against the civil rights activists who fought racial segregation in the 1960s.

The pro-choice movement supports FACE and credits it with reducing the number of violent clinic incidents during the past several years. In 1994, 67 percent of reproductive health clinics reported acts of violence, harassment, or intimidation, but by the year 2000, 44 percent of these clinics reported such incidents. Severe acts of violence were down to 20 percent of clinics in 2000, compared to 52 percent in 1994. Nevertheless, most abortion providers claim that they still experience the same amount of picketing, hate mail, and harassing phone calls. Some maintain that the decrease in violent incidents at clinics is due more to stepped-up police patrols at high-risk times (such as at the anniversary of *Roe v. Wade* and on weekends) than to the passage of FACE itself.

While most pro-choicers and pro-lifers agree that activists should be permitted to openly express their opposition to facilities that provide abortions, some disagree on the constitutionality and ethics of certain protest tactics. The cartoonists in the following chapter offer compelling opinions on this issue.

Examining Cartoon 1:
"It's in the Constitution Somewhere . . ."

About the Cartoon

In 1997, the U.S. Supreme Court upheld the Freedom of Access to Clinic Entrances Act (FACE), a law passed by Congress in 1994 that prohibited protesters from physically blockading abortion clinics. In another 1997 Supreme Court case, *Schenk v. Pro-Choice Network of New York*, the justices also upheld the "fixed buffer zone," a measure prohibiting all demonstration activity within fifteen feet of a clinic's doorways, driveways, or parking lot entrances. Some anti-abortion activists maintained that these Court rulings interfered with their right to freedom of expression. Abortion-rights supporters responded that such a freedom should not be used to deny a woman's right to reproductive choice.

Abortion protesters retained their right to picket outside of abortion clinics as long as they did not block entrances or violate the fixed buffer zone. And although the Court's *Schenk* decision prevented picketing within fifteen feet of a clinic, it struck down the "floating buffer zone"—a measure that had previously required demonstrators to stay at least fifteen feet away from any person or vehicle approaching or leaving the clinic. As long as protesters respect the fixed buffer zone, they may still picket, hand out leaflets, or talk with individuals on their way into an abortion clinic.

This cartoon expresses disagreement with the tactics of anti-abortion protesters and implicitly criticizes those who use the free speech argument to defend their decision to picket abortion clinics and providers. The cartoonist maintains that such "free speech" actually amounts to heckling and harassment.

About the Cartoonist

Herbert Block, the internationally syndicated cartoonist who drew under the pen name Herblock, regularly contributed political cartoons to the *Washington Post* from 1946 to 2001. Block was the winner of three Pulitzer Prizes for editorial cartooning and recipient of the 1994 Medal of Freedom, the highest civilian honor in the United States. Before his death in 2001, he was best known for his lampoons of U.S. presidents and for his comic commentary on the major social issues of his time.

Examining Cartoon 2:
"I Wish the Supreme Court Would Give *Me* a Protective Buffer Zone . . ."

About the Cartoon

In 1997, the Supreme Court upheld a lower court's ruling that created a "fixed buffer zone" prohibiting all protest demonstration activity within fifteen feet of an abortion clinic's doorways, driveways, and parking lot entrances.

The buffer zone is intended to protect women's access to reproductive health care clinics. The creator of this cartoon, however, maintains that it is actually the fetus that needs protection from abortion providers. The cartoon illustrates a certain kind of irony: The fetus is drawn inside the womb—a natural "protective buffer zone"—yet expresses feelings of vulnerability because the laws of the world in which it exists do not safeguard its right to life.

About the Cartoonist

Steve Breen, a native of Huntington Beach, California, studied political science at the University of California in Riverside. He became a cartoonist for New Jersey's *Asbury Park Press* in 1996, and was nationally syndicated in 1997. In 2001, he joined the staff of the *San Diego Union-Tribune* as a full-time editorial cartoonist. Breen won the 1998 Pulitzer Prize for editorial cartooning.

Examining Cartoon 3:
"Respect Life . . ."

About the Cartoon

This cartoon appeared in the wake of the 1998 murder of Barnett Slepian, a New York obstetrician who performed abortions. Slepian, who was shot from outside his kitchen window, had received death threats from radical abortion opponents since the 1980s. His homicide was one among several high-profile incidents of violence against abortion clinics and abortion providers during the 1990s. Eventually, anti-abortion activist James Kopp was arrested for Slepian's murder.

Pro-choice advocates have often criticized segments of the pro-life movement for inciting violence against abortion providers.

Abortion rights supporters contend that pro-lifers frequently use starkly moralistic language in their condemnation of abortion (such as "abortion is murder" or "abortion kills babies") that intentionally or unintentionally inspires extremists to take violent action against abortion providers. This cartoon focuses on the paradox inherent in the image of a threatening gunman who sports a hat featuring the pro-life injunction to "respect life." The implication is that those who condone the killing of abortion providers—including some members of the pro-life movement—have no real respect for life.

About the Cartoonist

Ben Sargent began his journalistic career as a reporter for the *Corpus Christi Caller Times* and United Press International. In 1974, he started drawing editorial cartoons for the *Austin American-Statesman*. Sargent is the recipient of several awards, including the 1982 Pulitzer Prize for editorial cartooning and the 1988 Free Press Association's Mencken Award. He is also the author of *Texas Statehouse Blues* and *Big Brother Blues*.

Sargent. © 1998 by the *Austin American-Statesman*. Reprinted by permission of Universal Press Syndicate.

Examining Cartoon 4:
"Violence! Violence!"

"VIOLENCE! VIOLENCE! ALWAYS VIOLENCE!! NOW WHO IS GOING TO KILL THIS KID FOR ME?!"

About the Cartoon

The pro-choice movement has frequently accused the pro-life movement of framing the abortion debate in a way that leads some activists to justify violence against abortion clinics and providers. This cartoon, however, suggests that pro-choicers who decry the bombings and arsons of abortion clinics are as violent—perhaps even more so—than those responsible for the destruction of clinics. In the artist's opinion, the pregnant woman looking at the burned-out abortion clinic is able to see the violence in the actions of those who attacked the clinic, but not the brutality in her own plans to "kill" her unborn child.

About the Cartoonist

M. Roche Brown has drawn cartoons for *Life Advocate*, a bimonthly pro-life magazine.

Organizations to Contact

The editors have compiled the following list of organizations concerned with the issues debated in this book. The descriptions are derived from materials provided by the organizations. All have publications or information available for interested readers. The list was compiled on the date of publication of the present volume; the information provided here may change. Be aware that many organizations take several weeks or longer to respond to inquiries, so allow as much time as possible.

ACLU Reproductive Freedom Project
125 Broad St., New York, NY 10004-2400
(212) 549-2500
e-mail: aclu@aclu.org • website: www.aclu.org

A branch of the American Civil Liberties Union, the project coordinates efforts in litigation, advocacy, and public education to guarantee the constitutional right to reproductive choice. Its mission is to ensure that reproductive decisions will be informed, meaningful, and free of hindrance or coercion from the government. The project disseminates fact sheets, pamphlets, and editorial articles. It also publishes the quarterly newsletter *Reproductive Rights Update*.

Alan Guttmacher Institute
120 Wall St., 21st Floor, New York, NY 10005
(212) 248-1111 • fax: (212) 248-1951
e-mail: info@agi-usa.org • website: www.agi-usa.org

The institute is a reproduction research group that advocates the right to safe and legal abortion. It provides extensive statistical information on abortion and voluntary population control. Publications include the bimonthly journal *Family Planning Perspectives*, which focuses on reproductive health issues; *Preventing Pregnancy, Protecting Health: A New Look at Birth Control in the U.S.*; and the book *Sex and America's Teenagers*.

American Life League (ALL)
PO Box 1350, Stafford, VA 22555
(540) 659-4171 • fax: (540) 659-2856
e-mail: whylife@all.org • website: www.all.org

ALL promotes family values and opposes abortion. The organization monitors congressional activities dealing with pro-life issues and provides information on the physical and psychological risks of abortion. It produces educational materials, books, flyers, and programs for profamily organizations that oppose abortion. Publications include the biweekly newsletter *Communique*, the bimonthly magazine *Celebrate Life*, and the weekly newsletter *Lifefax*.

Americans United for Life (AUL)
310 S. Peoria St., Suite 300, Chicago, IL 60604-3816
(312) 492-7234 • fax: (312) 492-7235
e-mail: infor.aul@juno.com • website: www.unitedforlife.org

AUL promotes legislation to make abortion illegal. The organization operates a library and a legal-resource center. It publishes the quarterly newsletter *Lex Vitae*, the monthly newsletter *AUL Insights* and *AUL Forum*, and numerous booklets, including *The Beginning of Human Life* and *Fetal Pain and Abortion: The Medical Evidence*.

Catholics for a Free Choice (CFFC)
1436 U St. NW, Suite 301, Washington, DC 20009
(202) 986-6093 • fax: (202) 332-7995
website: www.cath4choice.org

CFFC supports the right to legal abortion and promotes family planning to reduce the incidence of abortion and to increase women's choices in childbearing and child rearing. It publishes the bimonthly newsletter *Conscience,* the booklet *The History of Abortion in the Catholic Church,* and the brochure *You Are Not Alone.*

Center for Bio-Ethical Reform (CBR)
PO Box 8056, Mission Hills, CA 91346
(818) 360-2477 • fax: (818) 360-2477
e-mail: cbr@cbrinfo.org • website: www.cbrinfo.org

CBR opposes abortion, focusing its arguments on abortion's moral aspects. Its members frequently address conservative and Christian groups throughout the United States. The center also offers training seminars on fundraising to pro-life volunteers. CBR publishes the monthly newsletter *In-Perspective* and a student training manual for setting up pro-life groups on campuses titled *How to Abortion-Proof Your Campus.* Its audiotapes include "Is the Bible Silent on Abortion?" and "No More Excuses."

Childbirth by Choice Trust
344 Bloor St. West, Suite 306, Toronto, ON M5S 3A7 Canada
(416) 961-1507 • fax: (416) 961-5771
e-mail: info@cbctrust.com
website: www.cbctrust.com

Childbirth by Choice Trust's goal is to educate the public about abortion and reproductive choice. It produces educational materials that aim to provide factual, rational, and straightforward information about fertility control issues. The organization's publications include the booklet *Abortion in Law, History, and Religion* and the pamphlets *Unsure About Your Pregnancy? A Guide to Making the Right Decision* and *Information for Teens About Abortion.*

Feminist Majority Foundation (FMF)
1600 Wilson Blvd., Suite 801, Arlington, VA 22209
(703) 522-2214 • fax (703) 522-2219
e-mail: femmaj@feminist.org • website:www.feminist.org

FMF advocates political, economic, and social equality for women. The foundation also strives to protect abortion rights for women. It hosts the National Clinic Defense Project and the Campaign for RU-486 and Contraceptive Research. FMF reports on feminist issues, including abortion, in its quarterly *Feminist Majority Report.*

Feminists for Life of America
733 15th St. NW, Suite 1100, Washington, DC 20005
(202) 737-3352
e-mail: fems4life@aol.com • website: www.feministsforlife.org

This organization is comprised of feminists united to secure the right to life, from conception to natural death, for all human beings. It believes that legal abortion exploits women. The group supports a human life amendment, which would protect unborn life. Publications include the quarterly *Sisterlife*, the book *Prolife Feminism: Different Voices*, the booklet *Early Feminist Case Against Abortion*, and the pamphlet *Abortion Does Not Liberate Women*.

Human Life Foundation (HLF)
215 Lexington Ave., New York, NY 10016
(212) 685-5210 • fax: (212) 725-9793
website: www.humanlifereview.com

The foundation serves as a charitable and educational support group for individuals opposed to abortion, euthanasia, and infanticide. HLF offers financial support to organizations that provide women with alternatives to abortion. Its publications include the quarterly *Human Life Review* and books and pamphlets on abortion, bioethics, and family issues.

Human Life International (HLI)
4 Family Life Ln., Front Royal, VA 22630
(540) 635-7884 • fax: (540) 635-7363
e-mail: hli@hli.org • website: www.hli.org

HLI is a pro-life family education and research organization that opposes abortion. It offers positive alternatives to what it calls the antilife/antifamily movement. The organization publishes *Confessions of a Prolife Missionary*, *Deceiving Birth Controllers*, and the monthly newsletters *HLI Reports* and *Special Reports*.

National Abortion and Reproductive Rights Action League (NARAL)
1156 15th St. NW, Suite 700, Washington DC 20005
(202) 973-3000 • fax: (202) 973-3096
e-mail: naral@naral.org • website: www.naral.org

NARAL works to develop and sustain a pro-choice political constituency in order to maintain the right of all women to legal abortion. The league briefs members of Congress and testifies at hearings on abortion and related issues. It publishes the quarterly *NARAL Newsletter.*

National Coalition of Abortion Providers (NCAP)
206 King St., Alexandria, VA 22314
(703) 684-0055 • fax: (703) 684-5051
e-mail: ronncap@aol.com • website: www.ncap.com

NCAP is a pro-choice organization that represents the political interests of independent abortion providers nationwide. The coalition lobbies in Washington, D.C., for pro-choice, pro-provider policies. NCAP publishes the bimonthly newsletter *NCAP News.*

National Conference of Catholic Bishops (NCCB)
3211 Fourth St. NE, Washington, DC 20017-1194
(202) 541-3000 • fax: (202) 541-3054
website: www.nccbusc.org

The NCCB, which adheres to the Vatican's opposition to abortion, is the American Roman Catholic bishops' organ for unified action. Through its committee on pro-life activities, it advocates a legislative ban on abortion and promotes state restrictions on abortion, such as parental consent/notification laws and strict licensing laws for abortion clinics. Its pro-life publications include the educational kit *Respect Life* and the monthly newsletter *Life Insight.*

National Right to Life Committee (NRLC)
419 Seventh St. NW, Suite 500, Washington, DC 20004
(202) 626-8800
e-mail: nrlc@nrlc.org • website: www.nrlc.org

NRLC is one of the largest organizations opposing abortion. The committee campaigns against legislation to legalize abortion. It encourages ratification of a constitutional amendment granting embryos and fetuses the same right to life as living persons, and it advocates alternatives to abortion, such as adoption. NRLC publishes the brochure *When Does Life Begin?* and the *National Right to Life News.*

Planned Parenthood Federation of America (PPFA)
810 Seventh Ave., New York, NY 10019
(212) 541-7800 • fax: (212) 245-1845
e-mail: communication@ppfa.org
website: www.plannedparenthood.org

PPFA is a national organization that supports people's right to make their own reproductive decisions without governmental interference. It provides contraception, abortion, and family planning services at clinics located throughout the United States. Among its extensive publications are the pamphlets *Abortions: Questions and Answers, Five Ways to Prevent Abortion*, and *Nine Reasons Why Abortions Are Legal*.

Pro-Life Action League (PLAL)
6160 N. Cicero Ave., Suite 600, Chicago, IL 60646
(773) 777-2900 • fax: (773) 777-3061
e-mail: scheidler@ibm.net • website: www.prolifeaction.org

PLAL is a pro-life organization dedicated to ending abortion. Working through nonviolent direct action—particularly sidewalk counseling—the league actively protests abortion. Its website contains press releases related to PLAL's current campaigns and its efforts to maintain protesters' access to abortion clinics. Its student research section includes the articles "Back Alley Abortion" and "Sidewalk Counseling."

Religious Coalition for Reproductive Choice (RCRC)
1025 Vermont Ave. NW, Suite 1130, Washington, DC 20005
(202) 628-7700 • fax: (202) 628-7716
e-mail: info@rcrc.org • website: www.rcrc.org

RCRC consists of more than thirty Christian, Jewish, and other religious groups committed to helping individuals to make decisions concerning abortion in accordance with their conscience. The organization supports abortion rights, opposes anti-abortion violence, and educates policy makers and the public about the diversity of religious perspectives on abortion. RCRC publishes booklets, an education essay series, the pamphlets *Abortion and the Holocaust: Twisting the Language* and *Judaism and Abortion*, and the quarterly *Religious Coalition for Reproductive Choice Newsletter.*

For Further Research

Books

Randy Alcorn, *Prolife Answers to Prochoice Arguments*. Sisters, OR: Multnomah, 2000.

Hadley Arkes, *Natural Rights and the Right to Choose*. New York: Cambridge University Press, 2002.

Linda J. Beckman and S. Marie Harvey, eds., *The New Civil War: The Psychology, Culture, and Politics of Abortion*. Washington, DC: American Psychological Association, 1998.

Leslie Bonavoglia, ed., *The Choices We Made: Twenty-Five Women and Men Speak Out About Abortion*. New York: Four Walls Eight Windows, 2001.

David Boonin, *A Defense of Abortion*. New York: Cambridge University Press, 2002.

Leslie Cannold, *The Abortion Myth: Feminism, Morality, and the Hard Choices Women Make*. Middletown, CT: Wesleyan University Press, 2001.

Daniel A. Dombrowski and Robert Deltete, *A Brief, Liberal, Catholic Defense of Abortion*. Chicago: University of Illinois Press, 2000.

Cynthia Gorney, *Articles of Faith: A Frontline History of the Abortion Wars*. New York: Simon and Schuster, 1998.

George Grant, *Grand Illusions: The Legacy of Planned Parenthood*. Nashville: Cumberland House, 2000.

Edwin C. Hui, *At the Beginning of Life: Dilemmas in Theological Bioethics*. Downers Grove, IL: InterVarsity Press, 2002.

Peter Kreeft, *Three Approaches to Abortion: A Compassionate and Thoughtful Guide to the Most Controversial Issue Today*. San Francisco: Ignatius Press, 2002.

Deborah R. McFarlane and Kenneth J. Meier, *The Politics of Fertility Control: Family Planning and Abortion Policies in the American States*. New York: Seven Bridges, 2000.

Roy M. Mersky and Jill Duffy, eds., *A Documentary History of the Legal Aspects of Abortion in the United States*. Littleton, CO: Fred B. Rothman, 2000.

Linda S. Myrsiades, *Splitting the Baby: The Culture of Abortion in Literature and Law, Rhetoric and Cartoons*. New York: Peter Lang, 2002.

Rosemary Nossiff, *Before Roe: Abortion Policy in the States*. Philadelphia: Temple University Press, 2000.

Jerry Reiter, *Live from the Gates of Hell: An Insider's Look at the Anti-Abortion Movement*. Amherst, NY: Prometheus Books, 2000.

Rachel Roth, *Making Women Pay: The Hidden Costs of Fetal Rights*. Ithaca, NY: Cornell University Press, 1999.

Jean Reith Schroedel, *Is the Fetus a Person?: A Comparison of Policies Across the Fifty States*. Ithaca, NY: Cornell University Press, 2000.

Laurie Shrage, *Abortion and Social Responsibility: Depolarizing the Debate*. New York: Oxford University Press, 2002.

Rickie Solinger, ed., *Abortion Wars: A Half Century of Struggle, 1950–2000*. Berkeley: University of California Press, 1998.

Kevin Wm. Wildes and Alan C. Mitchell, eds., *Choosing Life: A Dialogue on* Evangelium Vitae. Washington, DC: Georgetown University Press, 1997.

Periodicals

Joyce Arthur, "Abortion Is Not a Form of Genocide," *Humanist*, July/August 2000.

Amy Bach, "No Choice for Teens," *Nation*, October 11, 1999.

Chris Black, "The Partial-Birth Fraud," *American Prospect*, September 24, 2001.

Jennifer Braunschweiger, "My Father Was a Rapist," *Glamour*, August 1999.

Diana Brown, "A Wiser View of Abortion," *Free Inquiry*, Winter 1999.

William F. Buckley, "Partial Democracy from the Court," *National Review*, July 31, 2000.

Joanne Byfield, "Which Choice? An Influential U.S.-Based Lobby Group Claims to Be Catholic, but a New Report Proves It Is Not," *The Report Newsmagazine*, January 21, 2002.

Gregg Easterbrook, "Abortion and Brain Waves," *New Republic*, January 31, 2000.

James K. Fitzpatrick, "A Pro-Life Loss of Nerve?" *First Things*, December 2000.

Clarke D. Forsythe, "Abortion Is Not a 'Necessary Evil,'" *Christianity Today*, May 24, 1999.

Nancy Gibbs, "The Pill Arrives," *Time*, October 9, 2000.

Cynthia Gorney, "Abortion Changes, but How Much?" *New York Times*, September 29, 2000.

Joan Greenwood, "The New Ethics of Abortion," *Journal of Medical Ethics*, October 2001.

Ed Griffin-Nolan, "Rival Camps in Abortion Debate Gather, See Progress in Dialogue," *National Catholic Reporter*, June 5, 1998.

William Norman Grigg, "The 'Unwanted' Child," *New American*, January 17, 2000.

Edna Wells Handy, "A Matter of Choice," *Essence*, March 2000.

Nat Hentoff, "A Pro-Life Atheist Civil Libertarian," *Free Inquiry*, Fall 2001.

Ann Hwang, "Exportable Righteousness, Expendable Women," *World Watch*, January/February 2002.

Carole Joffe, "Bush's Antichoice Assault," *Nation*, May 28, 2001.

Wendy Kaminer, "Abortion and Autonomy," *American Prospect*, June 5, 2000.

John F. Kavanaugh, "Killing Unborn Patients," *America*, February 19, 2000.

Frances Kissling, "The Place for Individual Conscience," *Journal of Medical Ethics*, October 2001.

J.M. Lawson Jr. and Ignacio Castuera, "We Should Trust Women to Do the Choosing," *Los Angeles Times*, June 23, 2000.

Peter J. Leithart, "Attacking the Tabernacle," *First Things*, November 1999.

John Leo, "An Unspoken Threat," *U.S. News & World Report*, June 10, 2002.

Frederica Mathewes-Green, "We Can Find Common Ground on Abortion," *U.S. Catholic*, January 1998.

Michael W. McConnell, "*Roe v. Wade* at Twenty-Five: Still Illegitimate," *Wall Street Journal*, January 22, 1998.

Mary Meehan, "ACLU v. Unborn Children," *Human Life Review*, Spring 2001.

Ms., "I Am an Abortion Doctor," June/July 1999.

Lorraine V. Murray, "The Least of These," *America*, January 22, 2001.

Danielle Ofri, "Common Ground," *Tikkun*, January/February 2002.

Katha Pollitt, "This Warning May Be Hazardous to Your Health," *Nation*, April 16, 2001.

Anna Quindlen, "RU-486 and the Right to Choose," *Newsweek*, October 9, 2000.

Hanna Rosin, "Pain, Penance, and RU-486," *Washington Post*, October 14, 2000.

William Saleton, "TRB from Washington: Life Time," *New Republic*, June 19, 2000.

Elizabeth Schulte, "The New Assault on a Woman's Right to Choose," *International Socialist Review*, June/July 2000.

Richard Shoenig, "The Idiot's Guide to Salvation," *Humanist*, January/February 2000.

Dan Sloan, "Basic Issues in the Abortion Debate," *Political Affairs*, July 1999.

Benjamin J. Stein, "A Golden Age for Thugs," *American Spectator*, May 1998.

Andrew Sullivan, "R U 4 Life," *Human Life Review*, Spring 2001.

John M. Swomley, "Abortion as a Positive Moral Choice," *Human Quest*, July/August 1999.

Gary Thomas, "Roe v. McCorvey," *Christianity Today*, January 12, 1998.

Liz Townsend, "Full-Term Baby Survives Abortion Attempt," *National Right to Life News*, August 12, 1998.

Michael M. Uhlmann, "A Right to a Dead Child?" *Crisis*, November 2000.

Susan E. Wills, "Clinical Psychosis," *National Review*, November 23, 1998.

Naomi Wolf, "Pro-Choice *and* Pro-Life," *New York Times*, April 3, 1997.

Wendy Wright, "Federal Government Should Not Be in the Business of Funding Abortion," *Insight*, October 24, 2001.

Index